SandCastle 3

Homophones

Who's On Whose Spot?

Mary Elizabeth Salzmann

Publishing Company

Published by SandCastle™, an imprint of ABDO Publishing Company, 4940 Viking Drive, Edina, Minnesota 55435.

Cover and interior photo credits: Artville, Digital Stock, Eyewire Images, PhotoDisc, Rubberball Productions

Library of Congress Cataloging-in-Publication Data

Salzmann, Mary Elizabeth, 1968-
    Who's on whose spot? / Mary Elizabeth Salzmann.
        p. cm. -- (Homophones)
    Includes index.
    Summary: Photographs and simple text introduce homophones, words that sound alike but are spelled differently and have different meanings.
    ISBN 1-57765-798-5
    1. English language--Homonyms--Juvenile literature. [1. English language--Homonyms.] I. Title. II. Series.

PE1595 .S29 2002
428.1--dc21

2001053303

The SandCastle concept, content, and reading method have been reviewed and approved by a national advisory board including literacy specialists, librarians, elementary school teachers, early childhood education professionals, and parents.

Let Us Know

After reading the book, SandCastle would like you to tell us your stories about reading. What is your favorite page? Was there something hard that you needed help with? Share the ups and downs of learning to read. We want to hear from you! To get posted on the ABDO Publishing Company Web site, send us email at:

sandcastle@abdopub.com

About SandCastle™

Nonfiction books for the beginning reader

- Basic concepts of phonics are incorporated with integrated language methods of reading instruction. Most words are short, and phrases, letter sounds, and word sounds are repeated.

- Book levels are based on the ATOS™ for Books formula. Other considerations for readability include the number of words in each sentence, the number of characters in each word, and word lists based on curriculum frameworks.

- Full-color photography reinforces word meanings and concepts.

- "Words I Can Read" list at the end of each book teaches basic elements of grammar, helps the reader recognize the words in the text, and builds vocabulary.

- Reading levels are indicated by the number of flags on the castle.

SandCastle uses the following definitions for this series:

- Homographs: words that are spelled the same but sound different and have different meanings. *Easy memory tip: "-graph"= same look*

- Homonyms: words that are spelled and sound the same but have different meanings. *Easy memory tip: "-nym"= same name*

- Homophones: words that sound alike but are spelled differently and have different meanings. *Easy memory tip: "-phone"= sound alike*

Look for more SandCastle books in these three reading levels:

Level 1 (one flag)	**Level 2** (two flags)	**Level 3** (three flags)

Grades Pre-K to K 5 or fewer words per page	**Grades K to 1** 5 to 10 words per page	**Grades 1 to 2** 10 to 15 words per page

who's

who is

whose

a word used to ask
who something
belongs to

Homophones are words that sound alike but are spelled differently and have different meanings.

These kids share a secret.

Who's whispering in whose ear?

They like to eat ice cream.

Who's wearing overalls?

Whose hair is braided?

Whose is in a ponytail?

They like to jump on the trampoline.

Who's jumping the highest?

It is a very sunny day.

Whose sunglasses are round?

They like to go sledding.

Who's sitting in the back of
the sled?

11

Whose shirt has blue and white stripes?

Who's wearing glasses?

They are playing in their driveway.

Who's dribbling the basketball?

They are best friends.

Whose arm is around whose shoulder?

They had fun horseback riding.

Who's giving the horse an apple?

They each have a balloon to play with.

Whose balloon is yellow?

These boys are playing baseball.

Who's sliding into third base?

They are wearing special dresses from Bali.

Whose dress has green sleeves?

They are working on a school project.

Who's pointing to the computer?

They are fishing at the lake.

Who's putting bait on
the hook?

Zach and his dad are swinging.

Who's sitting on top of the tire?
(Zach)

Words I Can Read

Nouns

A noun is a person, place, or thing

apple (AP-uhl) p. 15
arm (ARM) p. 14
back (BAK) p. 11
bait (BAYT) p. 20
balloon (buh-LOON) p. 16
base (BAYSS) p. 17
baseball (BAYSS-bawl) p. 17
basketball (BASS-kit-bawl) p. 13
boys (BOIZ) p. 17
computer (kuhm-PYOO-tur) p. 19
dad (DAD) p. 21
day (DAY) p. 10
dress (DRESS) p. 18
dresses (DRESS-ez) p. 18

driveway (DRIVE-way) p. 13
ear (IHR) p. 6
friends (FRENDZ) p. 14
fun (FUHN) p. 15
glasses (GLASS-iz) p. 12
hair (HAIR) p. 8
homophones (HOME-uh-fonez) p. 5
hook (HUK) p. 20
horse (HORSS) p. 15
ice cream (EYESS KREEM) p. 7
kids (KIDZ) p. 6
lake (LAKE) p. 20
meanings (MEE-ningz) p. 5
overalls (OH-vur-awlz) p. 7

ponytail (POH-nee-tayl) p. 8
project (PROJ-ekt) p. 19
school (SKOOL) p. 19
secret (SEE-krit) p. 6
shirt (SHURT) p. 12
shoulder (SHOHL-dur) p. 14
sled (SLED) p. 11
sleeves (SLEEVZ) p. 18
stripes (STRIPESS) p. 12
sunglasses (SUHN-glass-iz) p. 10
tire (TIRE) p. 21
top (TOP) p. 21
trampoline (tram-puh-LEEN) p. 9
word (WURD) p. 4
words (WURDZ) p. 5

Proper Nouns

A proper noun is the name
of a person, place, or thing

Bali (BAH-lee) p. 18   Zach (ZAK) p. 21

Pronouns

A pronoun is a word that replaces a noun

each (EECH) p. 16

it (IT) p. 10

something
(SUHM-thing) p. 4

they (THAY) pp. 7, 9, 11, 13, 14, 15, 16, 18, 19, 20

who (HOO) p. 4

whose (HOOZ) pp. 4, 6, 8, 10, 12, 14, 16, 18

Verbs

A verb is an action or being word

are (AR) pp. 5, 10, 13, 14, 17, 18, 19, 20, 21

ask (ASK) p. 4

belongs (bi-LONGZ) p. 4

dribbling
(DRIB-uhl-ing) p. 13

eat (EET) p. 7

fishing (FISH-ing) p. 20

giving (GIV-ing) p. 15

go (GOH) p. 11

had (HAD) p. 15

has (HAZ) pp. 12, 18

have (HAV) pp. 5, 16

is (IZ) pp. 4, 8, 10, 14, 16

jump (JUHMP) p. 9

jumping (JUHMP-ing) p. 9

like (LIKE) pp. 7, 9, 11

play (PLAY) p. 16

playing (PLAY-ing) pp. 13, 17

pointing (POINT-ing) p. 19

putting (PUT-ing) p. 20

riding (RIDE-ing) p. 15

share (SHAIR) p. 6

sitting (SIT-ing) pp. 11, 21

sledding (SLED-ing) p. 11

sliding (SLIDE-ing) p. 17

sound (SOUND) p. 5

spelled (SPELD) p. 5

swinging (SWING-ing) p. 21

used (YOOZD) p. 4

wearing (WAIR-ing) pp. 7, 12, 18

whispering
(WISS-pur-ing) p. 6

working (WURK-ing) p. 19

Adjectives

An adjective describes something

alike (uh-LIKE) p. 5

best (BEST) p. 14

blue (BLOO) p. 12

braided (BRAYD-ed) p. 8

different (DIF-ur-uhnt) p. 5

green (GREEN) p. 18

highest (HYE-est) p. 9

his (HIZ) p. 21

round (ROUND) p. 10

special (SPESH-uhl) p. 18

sunny (SUH-nee) p. 10

their (THAIR) p. 13

these (THEEZ) pp. 6, 17

third (THURD) p. 17

white (WITE) p. 12

yellow (YEL-oh) p. 16

Adverbs

An adverb tells how, when, or where something happens

differently (DIF-ur-uhnt-lee) p. 5

horseback (HORSS-bak) p. 15

very (VER-ee) p. 10

Contractions

A contraction is two words combined with an apostrophe

who's (HOOZ) pp. 4, 6, 7, 9, 11, 12, 13, 15, 17, 19, 20, 21

24